Wisdom & Wit FOR WINNING

one day at a time

JIM LILLARD

Wisdom & Wit FOR WINNING

one day at a time

JIM LILLARD

encounters
press
TULSA, OK

Published by Encounters Press

Inspiring Hearts & Transforming Souls; One Book at at Time.

Tulsa, Oklahoma. Printed in U.S.A.

In a world plagued by conflict, rapid change, and relentless pressures, we need books to help us unravel the confusion in an attempt to make sense of life.

The printed page, ebooks and other media published under the banner of Encounters Press are targeted to be on the front-lines. As publishers we want to be responsive to the issues that touch people's lives. One of our primary missions is to publish true human experiences reflecting tragedy to triumph, underdog victories and conquests over the impossible. Additionally, Encounters Press is providing church leaders with biblical, user-friendly materials that will assist them in their evangelistic, teaching, leadership training and discipleship efforts.

For a FREE CATALOG of resources from Encounters Press please email us at: **Info@EncountersPress.com.**

www.EncountersPress.com

Pastor and Author Jim Lillard is the founding Pastor of
House of the Lord Fellowship Church, in Austin, Texas.
He has remained the Senior Pastor for 38 years.
Pastor Jim and his wife, Lue, of 46 years, live in Austin,
Texas. They have one son, Stuart and a grandson, Elvis.
Pastor Jim is a Teacher and is busy about
The Master's business.
He strives to bring a word in season
and lift up the body of Christ.

www.hotlchurch.com

"We must allow the Word of God to confront us, to disturb our security, to undermine our complacency and to overthrow our patterns of thought and behavior."
—John R.W. Scott

"The Word of God softens every hardened heart."
—Lailah Gifty Akita

"Don't argue with a professor, but test everything he says in the light of God's Word."
—Billy Graham

"If you cut him, (John Bunyan) he'd bleed Scripture!"
—Charles Haddon Spurgeon

We now present:

Wisdom & Wit for Winning
one day at a time

Enjoy!

God is faithful.

His Word is True.

His Love fails not.

His promises are certain.

Now what was the problem?

*Bring a little joy
into someone's life today and
experience the fullness
that comes from lifting
their perspective.
Become an agent of change!*

There is more Hope
in one promise from God,
than there is in all imagined desires
man may formulate.
Pray the Word and you will be heard.

God,

whose Word is always good,

is seeking followers whose word

can also be trusted

as a tool of change in the world.

Use your words

in agreement with His Words

to be an agent of change...

The real and true joy of living
is not what you get out of it
but what you are able to put into it.
Bless someone today
with an unsuspecting
act of generosity!

The cares of this world come
as seeds of doubt,
attempting to separate us
from a promise of God.
At the very appearance of care
or concern, remember
the promise of God
and defeat the lie
before it can grow!

Our Lord and Redeemer said that
you will recognize a believer by their works.
Not by their resume, title or testimony;
but by "what they do."
Our deeds speak for us as to who
or whose we really are.

The goodness of the Lord
never ceases.
His mercies are new
every morning and daily
He loads us with blessings!
He will withhold no good thing
from those who walk in integrity
with Him. We've got it made!

The God of all creation
does not make mistakes.
The problems that drop into your life
are so you can use the tools in your
New Covenant tool chest
to overcome them!
Apply the Word ---
defeat the lie!

A person's character is seen
not when things are going good,
but when all seems to be
in opposition to them.
Hard times reveal character.
Win in every trial of life
and glorify your Father
in Heaven!

A Word from the Lord
is of more value
than a thousand thoughts
from one's understanding.
A wise person is quiet to listen for that
still small voice of the Spirit's leading.

You shall decree a thing
and it will be established for you,
and the light of the revelation
will shine upon your walk.
This is the way to rule
and reign under His Lordship.
Create something
with your words today!

Believers learn to develop
that third eye of the spirit,
so they can see through
the promises of God and not just
with natural comprehension or observation.

The number one cause of failure in accomplishment is failure in the process and preparation that leads to accomplishing a goal or thing. Success is built a step at a time; it is produced not discovered.

The greatest challenges we face
are the ones we let inside.
Keep the promises of God
between you and every temptation, test,
or trial that comes your way!

Belief is a starting place,
but it is trust that ensures
the outcome of life's challenges.
In whom have you vested
your trust?

Pursue life after the Spirit
and let the mind
deal with the simple stuff.

I wonder if people would
live their lives differently,
if they realized eternity begins
when they are birthed
into the world, and not when
they depart this earthly plane?

Negativity is a communicable disease
that drains one's faith
and cripples their future.
Stay positive and
avoid those who are not.

Ideas are the seeds from where
great fortunes grow.
God has put within you
all that you need to grow
the next abundant phase
of your life.
Reach into the storehouse of
His wisdom, deposited in you,
and draw out His plan
for your life.

God always brings the best
to those who pass the test
and overcome life's challenges.
The Winner in you is greater
than any lie that opposes you.

While the old adage,
"It takes more muscles to frown
than it does to smile," may be true,
the frown is natural to a fallen
world system. Therefore,
we must fight to overcome
the natural tendency.
So it is with faith!
We must fight to overcome the
natural weakness of doubt.
Now stand and win!!!

You were Created by God
to rule and reign over all
that will arise today.
You were born of Him
to represent His will in the earth.
Do not allow petty issues
to sidetrack you from the success
that is inherently yours!

*Miracles are the fruit
of believers who actively pursue
a promise of God's Word.*

Having done all necessary to stand,

we stand in faith knowing

His promises will never fail us

and we will not pull back

or hold back

from His Word.

Life can be mysterious,

even baffling;

until you recognize the

"Fathers' Original Intent,"

for man to rule and reign

in the risen Lord,

as kings and priests unto God.

If every believer

treated other believers

the way they themselves

want to be treated

how much stronger would

the Kingdom of God

be represented in the earth?

God only gives the best.
His intent for His people is the
abundant full and free life of joy
and peace. Refuse to settle for less.
His Word in our mouth
insures our victory!!!

Wishing can never do the work
that Faith was designed to do.
Fully trusting His Word
will bring the results He promised.

A promise from God
is more secure
than cash in your bank account
and is accessible
in much the same way.
Make a demand
on the promises in your
heavenly account!

As a child of The King,
every believer is an inheritor.
But how many ever read the Will
to see what they inherited.

Character is identified
in what a person does,
not in what they say or
what they may know.
No gift in a person's life
can make up for
what character lacks.

A true giver knows
it is not always what we give,
or to whom we give it,
but what is set in motion
because we gave
that brings us the greatest joy.

"The blessings of the Lord
make rich and add no sorrow."
If we believe His promise to us,
are we making room for the wealth
He has released to us?

For God so loved that He gave.
love prompts us to give.
That being said,
where does the prompting to withold,
come from?
Freely we have received
so freely give.

Great peace comes from knowing
He will never leave nor forsake us.
But when our plans
conflict with His will for us,
it is we who have left
and forsaken Him.
He is still there for us, back where
our will pulled us away from His.

People sometimes forget
            that a life of thanksgiving
begins an attitude of gratitude
            and not with words of platitude.

Encouragement.
It is such a big word
to describe a small act of kindness
that can lift our day
and lighten our load.
You are a blessing to me!

Our Redeemer lives
and wants to manifest His power,
presence and grace through us today.
Demonstrate His great love
in every encounter
to which you are led !

When life seems hardest,
we experience the greatest growth.
The troubles come
so that we can conquer them.
New victories bring new strength,
new wisdom and greater resolve
for the next set of challenges!

Grace is God's gift to man
that when activated
allows man to access the divine realm
of life and function!

Never forget,
God saw it coming before you did,
and He has already prepared
a way out for you.
Let faith show you the way!

Righteousness is God's gift of grace.

Thanksgiving is our response of praise.

Celebrate your freedom today!

Goals, planning, and
commitment, are essential
for a successful life.
When we plan to succeed
we engage a process
that leads to triumph.

Courage is a force for good
that must be surrendered to
in order to be empowered by.
What a great season to "take" courage
and do deeds larger than self!

Two thousand years ago,
the Church was birthed in the
power and presence
of the Holy Spirit.
Today we celebrate His coming
and anticipate His manifestation
that we may be His vessels of
Kingdom power and might!

Miracles still happen
to remind us that we are not limited
by facts and that His power
is still greater than our need!

Within every New Covenant
promise of our Lord,
is the power to produce itself.
He said it, we receive it
as a personal possession,
then we celebrate and give praise
for it and it comes to pass.
Do not grow weary in the process!

The greatest rewards in life,

come not from what we get out of it,

but what we put into it !

Life is a series of ongoing
challenges that are to be answered
with the Word of Truth.
The more victories we win,
the easier it becomes to win.
His grace is more than enough
to defeat every challenge!

Goals, planning, and commitment,

are essential to a successful life.

When we plan to succeed

we engage a process

that leads to triumph.

I am so glad
that I do not have to qualify for
the grace our Lord freely gives,
and yet, it is sufficient for every
need that may arise.
I can do all things through
His anointing that infuses me
with divine ability.

The words FAITH and TRUST
are synonymous when receiving from God.
To trust God and His promises
regardless of all else is a stand of Faith.

Our brain needs
intellectual input to grow
and remain healthy.
Our spirit man requires
spiritual input from the Word
and the Spirit.
Continually grow and
expand your ability to be used
of the Father in either realm.

While some levels
of intelligence acquired,
can be measured by a test,
the real measure is best seen
in what they accomplish
and leave behind for others.

The beauty of a wild flower
is not diminished by the fact
it was not cultivated or that
it grows among weeds
at the road side.
Its beauty is
even more pronounced because it
stands out against
its surroundings.
Let the beauty of our Lord
be seen in you, surrounded by
the world. Shine outside church!

With all that is going on in the world,
isn't it good to know
that we have direct access to
the highest power?
Keep the switch of Faith turned on!

A good man falls seven times
but gets up eight.
To the natural mind
the fall matters but to God.
The getting up after the fall
is what really matters.
Rise up from every fall
and start again;
God's got your back!

A miracle is simply
        an earth level look into
                "as it is in Heaven"
where that is the normal flow.

First thing every morning
God gives you a fresh,
clean day on which to write your
accomplishments and plans.
Do something big and bold!

The very worst day
in the kingdom of light,
is much better than the very best day
in the kingdom of darkness.
Let your light shine bright!

If life is what you make it,
why do so many seemingly busy
people not have a life of enjoyment?
Could there be elements of a
blessed and happy life that work
alone can never deliver?
He came that we might have and
enjoy life to the fullest.
He did the hard work and heavy
lifting, so that we could freely
receive the life He earned for us.

Trust in The Lord with all your
decision-making mechanism's
and do not try to figure out
with your mind,
what is going on,
and He will direct your path
and you will have great success!

There is a stirring
in the natural realm
that will have implications in the
realm of the Spirit.
Many will be caught off guard
while others are anxiously
awaiting this eminent blessing.
He is faithful who has promised,
and the flood tide is on the way!

A good thought is like a piece of clay;
the beginning of something useful.
It must be molded, shaped,
and brought to completion.
Despise not small beginnings.
Develop those thoughts.

Worry creeps in
when we forget a promise
of God's provision.
When His Word is held
as final authority
there is no fear.
Feed your faith—starve the doubt.

A mind and heart yielded to God,
His Word, His Spirit, and His power,
leads such an individual to a position of
purpose and influence
that cannot be denied.
Hear and win!

*Meditating on a promise
from God's Word
stretches a person to actually see
themselves in that promise and its
provision. See the Word,
be the Word, do the Word,
set the captives free!*

A person's real character

is seen not when things are going good,

but when all seems to be

in opposition to them.

Hard times reveal character.

Win in every trial of life.

Truth is not just
an accurate or factual statement;
truth is what God has said.
It may defy facts or even
observation, but trusting in His
Word will produce the fruit of
what He has said.

Faith takes ownership of a promise,
while hope tries to believe
it can happen!

In the world,
it gets messy
and is sometimes desolate.
But the God who corrected
creation with a word, is at our side
with the Word we need.

Victory must be experienced in one's mind before it can be achieved in one's life.

Life's biggest challenge
is not death, but rather
regret, for not having lived
it to its fullest.
Embrace all the fullness
life has to give!

Faith acted upon
is the match that ignites
the fire of Miracles.

Sense level wisdom is derived on a mental level from observation, study, experience, and experimentation, in the secular/ natural arena.

Godly wisdom is far superior and is downloaded from the Spirit of Truth and allows the Believer to know in their spirit, what their mental faculties could never comprehend.

Winning starts with attitude.
It is hard to experience success
while fearing failure.

Eventually,
everyone is faced with
the question "Why am I here?"
Only those who understand
original intent are equipped
to answer truthfully.

Time should be measured
in experiences embraced,
not in minutes or hours expended.
The best of life is always ahead, not behind.

A new day dawns and
a new chance unfolds
to accomplish things
that have yet to be done.
What we do with today
will lay the foundation for what
we can accomplish with our
tomorrows.

The Salvation Prayer

Whoever you are, whatever your current situation, no matter if you are in trouble or at the end of your rope; God loves you. Regardless if you are a student, businessman or business woman, housewife, C.E.O. or professional, God loves you right now. There is nothing you can do to earn more of His love. God did the ultimate thing for you and me; He gave His only begotten Son as a sacrifice for ALL of our sin—now that's some real love! Not only did Jesus lay down His life and die, but He also rose up from the dead as a sign and wonder so that we could spend eternity with Him in Heaven and experience an abundant life here on earth. If you are tired of the way your life has been going and need a fresh start— if you are filled with emptiness, darkness or constant sadness and need someone to believe in you and give you a second chance, then it is time for you to ask Jesus Christ into your heart and life—to take over and give you peace, direction and purpose! Just say out loud, the following prayer of salvationand mean it with all of your heart:

"Heavenly Father, I come to You in the Name of Your Son Jesus Christ. You said in Your Word that "*Whosoever shall call upon the name of the Lord shall be saved,*" (Romans 10:13). Father, I am calling on Jesus right now. I believe He died on the cross for my sins, that He was raised from the dead on the third day, and He's alive right now. Lord Jesus, I am asking You now, come into my heart. Live Your life in me and through me. I repent of my sins and surrender myself totally and completely to You. Heavenly Father, by faith I now confess Jesus Christ as my new Lord and from this day forward, I dedicate my life to serving Him."

If you prayed this prayer to receive Jesus Christ as your Savior for the very first time, please let us know on the "Contact Us" page at **www.HOTLchurch.com** and we will send you a great book and other information to help you get started in your new life in Christ - FREE of charge, of course. We are excited for your future! Well done.

Please include your prayer requests when you write.

_____

_____

_____

_____

_____

_____

_____

_____

_____

_____

_____

_____

_____

_____

_____

_____

Encounters Press—
Inspiring Hearts & Transforming Souls; One Book At A Time!

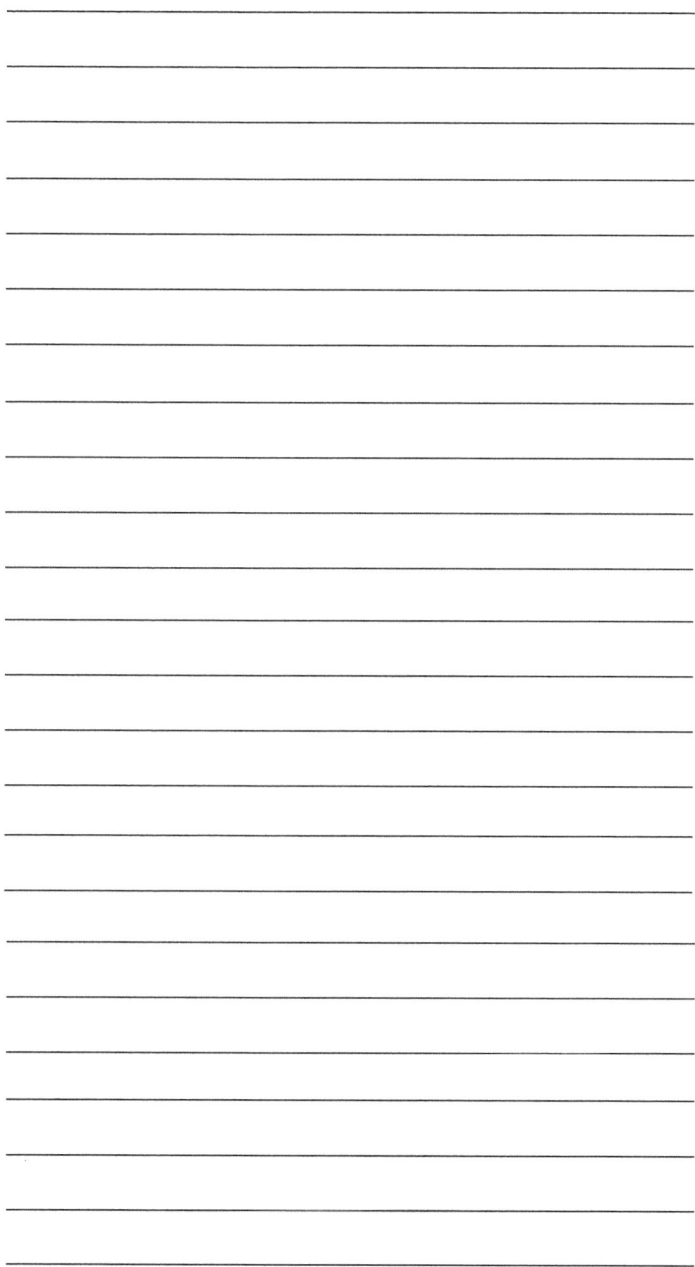

www.ingramcontent.com/pod-product-compliance
Lightning Source LLC
Chambersburg PA
CBHW071619040426
42452CB00009B/1394